Goodness Graces!

Goodness Graces!

Ten Short Stories about the Sacraments

By Diana R. Jenkins

auline
BOOKS & MEDIA
Boston

Nihil Obstat: Rev. Thomas W. Buckley, STD, SSL

Imprimatur: ✠Seán P. Cardinal O'Malley, OFM Cap.
Archbishop of Boston
December 3, 2009

Library of Congress Cataloging-in-Publication Data

Jenkins, Diana R.
  Goodness graces! ten short stories about the Sacraments / by Diana R. Jenkins.
      p. cm.
  ISBN 0-8198-3110-7 (pbk.)
  1. Sacraments--Catholic Church--Juvenile literature. 2. Catholic Church--
Doctrines--Juvenile literature. I. Title.
  BX2200.J46 2010
  234'.16088282--dc22
                        2009052222

Cover art by Veronica Walsh

Design by Mary Joseph Peterson, FSP

Published by Pauline Books & Media, 50 Saint Pauls Avenue, Boston, MA 02130-3491. www.pauline.org.

Printed in the U.S.A.

GGCS VSAUSAPEOILL06-10J10-03253 3110-7

Pauline Books & Media is the publishing house of the Daughters of St. Paul, an international congregation of women religious serving the Church with the communications media.

1 2 3 4 5 6 7 8 9   13 12 11 10

The Catholic Quick Reads Series

Contents

What Are the Seven Saraments?

Jesus gave the Church seven special gifts called sacraments. Through water, bread, wine, oil, gestures, and words, we are touched by Jesus' saving death and resurrection. The sacraments give us grace—a sharing in God's life. They make us holy.

The sacraments don't just represent or symbolize the ways God is present to us. What they represent actually becomes reality. For example, during the Eucharist, bread and wine actually *become* the Body and Blood of Jesus, although they still look and taste like bread and wine. When we receive the sacrament

of Reconciliation, we are actually forgiven by
God. Through the sacraments, Jesus teaches us
about himself and helps us to live what we have
learned. The sacraments join us with Jesus and
with other Catholics around the world, uniting
us as the Body of Christ.

The Sacraments of Initiation

Baptism, Confirmation, and Eucharist are
called Sacraments of Initiation because they are
the beginning and foundation of the Christian
life. They bring us into the Church and make us
Christ's followers and witnesses.

Baptism

In the sacrament of Baptism, we are united
to Jesus and become part of the Church,
the Body of Christ. Baptism is a sacrament
we receive only once. It marks us forever as
children of God. At Baptism, we are washed
free of original sin, and our personal sins (in the
case of a person old enough to commit sin) are
also forgiven. Catholics are usually baptized as
infants, but can be baptized at any age. By the

action of the Holy Spirit, we become alive with the life of the risen Jesus and are able to receive the other sacraments.

Confirmation

Confirmation is related to the sacrament of Baptism. When we are confirmed, the power of the Holy Spirit brings about a deeper sharing in Christ's mission. The confirmed person is called to become more committed to Jesus Christ and is strengthened to live as his follower. Baptism unites us to Jesus, and Confirmation sends us out in his name.

Eucharist

The third sacrament of initiation, and the most important sacrament of all, is the Eucharist. In the Eucharist, we join with Jesus as we remember how he gave himself for love of us, dying on the cross and then rising from the dead. As he told us to, we offer bread and wine, which, through the power of the Holy Spirit, become the Body and Blood of Christ. Each time we receive him in Holy Communion, God's life in us is strengthened.

The Sacraments of Healing

There are two sacraments that bring healing, each in a different way and for different situations. They are the sacraments of Reconciliation and Anointing of the Sick.

Reconciliation

Reconciliation offers us a special kind of healing: the healing of our relationship with God and with the Church, which we break when we sin.

When we confess our sins to a priest, we admit to God, to ourselves, and to the Church that we have made some wrong choices. We make a decision to do better. When the priest says the words of absolution, we see in him the forgiving love of Jesus. The penance assigned to us helps us to make up for the wrong we have done by sinning.

Anointing of the Sick

Anointing of the Sick is offered to those who are very ill. This sacrament may be celebrated at Mass, at the home of the sick person, or in a hospital. The sick person is anointed with oil, and the priest prays for his or her health.

The grace of this sacrament helps the sick person in many ways. It gives strength, peace, and courage, helping the person not to be discouraged by illness. It brings the spiritual healing of forgiveness of sins and sometimes brings physical healing, if that is God's will for the person. Anyone who has a serious illness or is becoming frail from old age may receive this sacrament, and it can be repeated if the person recovers and becomes sick again. This sacrament is especially consoling to the dying. The Anointing is a special blessing that accompanies them into eternal life.

The Sacraments of Commitment and Service

The last two sacraments, the sacraments of Matrimony and Holy Orders, give the person who receives them a particular mission in the Church—a mission of service to others.

Matrimony

Most people are called by God to be married. Husbands and wives serve Christ and the Church by serving each other and their children. In the celebration of the sacrament, the bride and bridegroom actually give the sacrament to each other. Before the Church, they promise to love and to be faithful to one another until death. The grace they receive in the sacrament gives them strength as they live their lives together. It helps them to form a family of faith and witness. Their love becomes a clear sign of the love between Jesus and his Church.

Holy Orders

Through the sacrament of Holy Orders, men are ordained as bishops, priests, or deacons to share in the ministry of Jesus. Each of these carries out a different role as they serve the Church. One of the most important ways they serve the Church is by administering the sacraments.

Bishops possess the fullness of the priesthood. They are the successors of Jesus' apostles. In union with the pope and all the other bishops, they bear responsibility for the whole Church, helping us all to grow in holiness. It is a bishop who administers the sacrament of Holy Orders and, usually, the sacrament of Confirmation.

Priests work alongside the bishops. They celebrate the sacraments, especially Eucharist and Reconciliation, proclaim the Gospel, preach, and guide us in the Church.

Deacons assist the bishops in their work, especially in baptizing, proclaiming the Gospel, and helping in ministries of charity.

Just Like Me

Waiting month after month for Mom to have her baby drove me nuts! I just knew that being a big sister would be so great. I imagined myself with the baby—reading, playing, teaching, getting really close. I figured that the baby's first word would be "Nicki." My name!

But when Mom and Dad brought home Grace (a sister!), things weren't exactly the way I thought they'd be.

For one thing, I just didn't realize how really tiny and delicate babies were! I had to be so careful with Grace, handling her ve-e-ery gently.

I was afraid that I'd hurt her just by picking her up!

I thought that playing with a baby would be fun, but you couldn't really play with Grace. I tried peek-a-boo with her, but she didn't react. She didn't understand it, I guess, but it wasn't like it was the most complicated game in the world!

"Keep trying," Dad told me. "She'll get it! It took a while for you to get the idea when you were a baby."

But playing peek-a-boo all by yourself gets boring. So mostly I "played" with Grace by letting her hold my finger. At least she could do that! "You used to love it when people did that to you, too," Mom told me every time she saw me doing it.

The one thing Grace was good at was crying! She couldn't say what was wrong, so the reason *why* she was crying was always a big mystery. Did she need her diaper changed? Was she hungry? Did her big sister's face scare her? Who knew?

"What's she crying about?" I kept asking Mom and Dad.

"I don't know," said Mom. "You were like that, too."

"You know what?" said Dad. "She sounds just the way you did when you cried."

"Fascinating," I muttered.

I guess you can tell that I was disappointed in my little sister. All my dreams of a special relationship with her seemed stupid now. She couldn't *do* anything. Not one thing. I never imagined how totally helpless she would be!

I guess that helplessness is the reason why people have to pay so much attention to babies. I don't want to sound jealous, but when I became a big sister, I started to feel invisible. Mom and Dad were always busy with the baby. And everyone who visited practically ran over me to get to Grace.

One day Grandma came over, kissed me quickly, and hurried to see Mom and Grace in the sunroom. Grandma had cleaned and ironed the white dress that Grace would wear at her

Baptism. Mom and I had both worn it when we were babies. (Not that we could remember!)

"She'll look like an angel," said Grandma, showing the dress to Mom.

"She certainly will!" said Mom. Then they started talking about their plans for the special day, totally ignoring me! I slipped out of the room and went upstairs to do some homework. Later, I looked out the window and saw that Grandma was leaving. She'd hardly even spoken to me!

I stomped downstairs and into the sunroom. "Grandma didn't say good-bye!" I cried.

"Hush, Nicki," said Mom. "I just got Grace to sleep."

"But, Mom—" I started to say more, but guess who woke up just then and started bawling? "Sorry," I muttered, not really feeling very sorry at all.

"She's just learning how to get to sleep," said Mom. "Noises make it hard for her. As I recall, you were pretty sensitive—"

"—Please, Mom," I interrupted. "Don't tell me again how Grace is just like I was when

I was a baby." What difference did it make if Grace was just like me? So I was a pain, too. That didn't make things better now.

All our family and friends came to Grace's Baptism. As we waited outside the church, people kept saying that Grace looked just like me in the white dress. *So?* I thought (but didn't say). Then Father Williams let us into the church, and we all gathered around the baptismal font. Aunt Evie and Uncle Mike stood near Mom and Dad because they were going to be Grace's godparents, like Aunt Frances and Uncle Trevor were mine.

Father welcomed us and said, "It seems like only yesterday that we were having Nicki's Baptism." Everyone smiled at me. "What a special day that was! But then, it's always wonderful to welcome a new child of God into our church family."

That's when Grace started crying. Her wails echoed through the church like a fire alarm.

"Just like her big sister!" said Father Williams.

Everyone laughed, and I turned red. Why did people keep talking about how my little

sister was like me? I wasn't a baby anymore, so
what did it matter that I used to be?

But it was as if Father Williams heard my
question, because the next thing he said seemed
like an answer. "And before we know it, little
Grace will be a responsible and capable young
lady, just like her sister. Her parents, her family,
all of you will help her become that person. You
will help her grow as a child of God, nurturing
this new life in Christ that she now receives."

Then it hit me: even though I had been
just as helpless as Grace, I could now do a
million and one things. I had learned so much
in my life—and Grace would, too. I just had
to give her the same help, the same chances,
the same love that everyone else had given me.
My parents and godparents, our family and
friends had taught me the skills that I needed
in life—*and* they had helped me grow in my
relationship with God.

Grace is *like me!* I thought. *She's starting out
in life just like I did. Mom and Dad are giving
her the same gift they gave me: the gift of our*

faith. And she has all these people who care
about her, just like they care about me.

While Father Williams started the ceremony,
I looked around at everybody. They seemed
so happy to be involved in this day. It was as
if they couldn't wait to be part of Grace's life. I
realized that I felt the same way.

Grace screamed when Father Williams
poured the water on her head, which reminded
me that no matter how cool it was, raising a
baby wasn't going to be easy. Still, I felt glad
that I would get to be a big sister.

And who knows? Maybe Grace's first word
will be "Nicki!"

Questions to Think and Talk About

Just Like Me

1. Why was Nicki jealous of her little sister?

2. Make a list of all the people who care about you. How have these people helped you make it through life and grow in your relationship with God?

3. At Baptism, your parents chose Christianity for you. What decisions about your faith are you making for yourself now?

4. Nicki realized that being a big sister would be difficult, but wonderful, too. What similar challenges have you faced?

Time for a Change

First, Dad changed jobs.

Then we changed houses.

And schools!

"Maybe things will settle down now," I told my older brother, Jonas, as we headed off for the first day at our new school.

"I don't know, Austin," he said. "Change never changes."

"Uh . . . sure," I said.

"You know what I mean," he said. "Things are always changing."

"Well, they can stop now. I'm tired of changes."

"But if things stopped changing then that would *be* a change, so things wouldn't actually change at all."

"Uh-huh," I said. Then I changed the subject!

Of course, Jonas was right. (I hate it when that happens.) The changes didn't stop! Just as we were getting adjusted to the new school, our parents zapped us again.

"We have some good news," said Dad. "We're going back to church."

"We've really missed it," said Mom. "And we want you guys to experience being part of a church family."

My parents hadn't been to church for years, and Jonas and I had never gone at all. I was afraid this might be a hard change to handle—and I was right! There were great people and good activities at church, but I had trouble getting into the Mass. I missed sleeping in on Sundays. And there was a lot of stuff I didn't understand, which made it hard to pay attention. My parents read the Bible with us at home, so I was able to get something out of the readings . . . when I listened to them. But mostly Mass seemed like a waste of time.

Of course, I didn't say that to my parents. They were happy to be back at church, and I knew they hoped Jonas and I would like it.

"I wish they'd change their minds about *this*," I whispered to Jonas at Mass one Sunday.

"Me, too," he said.

Dad frowned at us, so we faced forward and put on interested expressions.

After going to Mass for a while, things did get better, which meant we didn't always have to *pretend* to be interested. Father Perez gave some pretty good talks about the readings. He even told a few jokes! We got familiar with the different parts of the Liturgy, and we started to understand what was going on. The singing and praying were kind of nice. I started to see why people feel closer to God when they're in church.

But even though we were getting more out of Mass, Jonas and I couldn't participate fully, because we'd never been baptized. Luckily, we could do something about that. There were classes for kids like us—classes to teach us about the faith and prepare us for Baptism.

In our first class, Mrs. Dundee, the teacher, passed out books and gave everybody an overview of the class. "Baptism is a very important sacrament," she told us. "It's through Baptism that we become children of God."

That sounded great, but then I realized something. If Baptism was going to make me a child of God, did that mean that God didn't really care about me right now? I thought things were okay between me and God, but now I figured maybe I didn't mean as much to him as I thought. It was a good thing I could be baptized and change how God felt about me!

But first there was a lot to learn. Mrs. Dundee sent us home with instructions to read the first chapter in our book. Then she spent the next class teaching us about Adam and Eve and original sin. In the class after that, we learned about Jesus' Baptism.

"Jesus didn't have any sins to be washed away," Mrs. Dundee said. "But we do."

I wanted to hurry up and get rid of my sins so I'd finally be somebody to God. But we were only on the third chapter of our book. It didn't look like I was going to change my relationship with the Lord any time soon—which really worried me, to tell you the truth.

"Do we have to keep going to that class?" I asked my parents one night at supper.

"Is there a problem?" asked Dad.

"Nope," said Jonas. "It's a really good class for learning stuff."

He was right—again—but that wasn't the point. "We *are* learning a lot," I said. "But I want to be baptized now!"

Mom laughed and put a hand over her heart. "Oh, Austin! I didn't know this meant so much to you."

"Neither did I," Jonas muttered.

"Well, it's a big deal," I said. Of course, Baptism meant a lot to me. How else was I going to become a child of God?

"Baptism *is* important," said Dad. "That's why you need classes to prepare for it."

I couldn't think of any way to argue with that, so I had to continue the classes. I tried to stay patient, but I got more and more frustrated about the situation. When Mrs. Dundee started teaching about our responsibilities as baptized Christians, I blurted out, "Can't we learn that stuff after we actually *are* baptized Christians?"

"He's really excited about getting baptized," explained Jonas. "Which is ironic. He doesn't usually like changes, but now he can't wait for a big change like Baptism." He turned to me. "You've changed, man."

"Whatever," I said. "All I know is I need to be baptized. Like yesterday!" Then I realized that sounded kind of desperate so I added, "I mean . . . Baptism is a really important sacrament."

"I appreciate your enthusiasm, Austin," said Mrs. Dundee. "But we have to be sure you understand all the different aspects of the faith, that you're making a real commitment to live the Gospel, that you're ready—"

"I'm ready already!" I cried. Mrs. Dundee frowned, so I added more calmly, "But I guess I can learn more."

As she turned back to the board, I slumped in my seat. I'd wasted so much of my life not being important to God. And now I had to waste more time?

When we got outside after class, Jonas demanded, "What's the matter with you?"

"What's the matter with *you*?" I said. "And everybody else in that class?"

Jonas folded his arms. "What are you talking about?"

"We're not children of God!" I cried.

"Well, we're not baptized yet, if that's what you mean," he said.

"But it's like you don't even care how God feels about you," I said. "Or you just don't get it. We're really not that important to God right now. And the only way to make him change his mind about us is to get baptized."

"Dude," said Jonas, "we can't *make* God do anything. God's . . . you know . . . God."

I wasn't getting through to him at all, and I felt too discouraged to talk about it anymore. Luckily, Mom drove up then, ending our conversation.

I was still feeling down at supper that night. Then Dad made me feel worse. "We have some good news," he said.

Oh, no, I thought. *Not another change!*

It turned out I was right, but in a good way. "I'm going to have a baby," announced Mom.

Everybody got really excited, and we all started talking at once. When things quieted down, Mom smiled and said, "We are so blessed. God loves us, and he loves this baby, too."

"Already?" I asked.

"Sure," said Dad. "God loves us even before we're born."

"Even before we're baptized?"

"Well, of course, Austin," he explained. "God made us, and Baptism is his gift of grace to us—because he loves us."

I had heard that plenty of times before, but now Baptism was on my mind, and I realized something. God loves everybody from the very beginning—which meant I was *already* important to God. Baptism wasn't going to change God's love. It wasn't going to *make* God love me—because he already did. Baptism wasn't going to change God at all!

While my family chattered around me, I thought about what I'd learned about Baptism: how it takes away sin and gives us grace and all that. I hadn't paid much attention in class today, but I did remember Mrs. Dundee talking about serving others and spreading our faith after we were baptized. I guess that's what she meant by "living the Gospel." I thought God would change after my baptism. (Duh! Like Jonas said: God is God.) But I was the one who was going to change!

"Wow," I said right out loud. I actually felt excited about being baptized and becoming that new person. I couldn't wait to become a child of God—and not in a freaked-out, panicky way.

Jonas looked at me. "Nothing ever stays the same for us, does it?"

For once, my brother was wrong. (Yes!) Everything might be completely different next week—and it probably would be!—but there was one thing we could always count on. That was God's love.

Hey, some things never change!

Questions to Think and Talk About

Time for a Change

1. Baptism is the first step on our faith journey. What other big steps have you taken in your relationship with God?

2. Have you ever been confused by something you learned about your faith? What did you do about it?

3. Does knowing that God loves everyone change your view of other people? How about people you don't like?

4. When you're impatient for something to happen, how do you deal with your frustration?

5. How have your parents' decisions affected your family and your life?

Same Old, Same Old

"Pssst! Callie . . . . *Callie!*"

Don't you hate it when someone interrupts a daydream? I was so annoyed with my little sister, Rose, for hissing at me that I snapped, "What do you want?"

Then I remembered I was in church.

Luckily, it was time for the sign of peace, so my voice didn't stick out like it would have at a quieter time. *Unluckily*, my parents were frowning at me. I hid my embarrassment by hugging Rose. Then I shook the hands of the people behind me.

When I turned back to hug Mom, she whispered, "Quit daydreaming."

"Yes, ma'am," I said.

I shouldn't have zoned out at Mass, but it wasn't the first time. I didn't pay much attention in church anymore. It was just the same old, same old thing every time!

After Mass, Uncle Chris came up to us outside the church. "Isn't there a special day coming up next month?" he joked. "Now, let me see . . . what is it?" Like Rose hadn't been talking our ears off for weeks!

"It's my first Communion!" Rose cried. "And it's special because I'm going receive Jesus, and all of the family will be with me, and I'll get to wear my white dress, and it's . . . "

"Don't worry, honey," said Uncle Chris with a laugh. "I'll be there!"

"Good!" said Rose. "Do you want to hear our song? We've been practicing every day."

"Don't we need to get going?" I asked.

Dad agreed, so we said our good-byes and went to our car. I could hardly wait to get home, change clothes, and head out for our first picnic hike of the spring. It's a Sunday tradition with our family, and I love it!

I was so glad to be out of church that I didn't mind Rose singing her first Communion song in the car. At first. But by the time we got to the park, I was sick of her screechy voice screeching on and on about a "new life with Jesus."

"Give it a rest, will you?" I said as we pulled into the parking lot.

"Callie!" scolded Dad.

"Well, we've heard that same old song a million times," I grumbled.

We ate our picnic out by the lake the way we always do. It was great being together and talking to each other. After our usual dessert of Dad's world-famous brownies, we hiked our favorite path through the woods.

Rose walked next to me, still talking nonstop about her first Communion. After she told me three times how special it was, I got irritated and said, "Big deal! I receive Communion every Sunday, you know."

"I know!" squealed Rose. "And I'll get to do that, too!"

"So?" I said. "It's just the same old, same old thing."

Rose laughed. "That's not true. They told us it's a special time with God."

"Whatever," I said coldly. But inside I was thinking that Communion should be special, like Rose said. But how could something feel special when you did it again and again?

Over the next week, Rose called all our family and friends and explained Holy Communion to them as if they'd never heard of it before!

"Rose, you don't have to tell people about the bread becoming Jesus," I said when she hung up from talking to Aunt Vickie. "They know that already!"

"I'm just reminding them," said Rose as she dialed again. "Now I'm going to call Grandma."

I went to our room so I wouldn't have to be "reminded," too. I already knew all about Holy Communion. I didn't need to hear about it from Rose.

The next few Sundays, I tried to pay better attention at Mass, but my mind kept wandering to what I'd be doing afterward. All week long our family members were busy with different activities. Our Sundays in the park were our *one time* to be together.

I couldn't wait for Rose's first Communion day to come and go. I'd be glad when it was over! I got so tired of hearing about how the bread would really be Jesus, and she would get closer to God, and wear her white dress, and everybody would be there with her, and blah, blah, blah. It was all true, but it was so annoying that she said the same old stuff over and over!

When the big morning came, Rose danced all over our room, driving me nuts. She even started screeching out this made-up song: "Special, special, special! It's a special day!"

I couldn't take it anymore. "Be quiet!" I shouted. Then when she did, I said, "Look, there's Communion at every Mass *every Sunday*. It's not that special, okay?"

"Yes, it is," she insisted.

"Use your head, Rose," I said. "Something that you do again and again can't be special."

Things got quiet. Suddenly, Rose said, "You mean . . . like our Sunday picnics?"

"No, that's different," I snapped.

"But we do it again and again." She started chanting, "We get in the car. We drive to the park. We eat by the lake. We—"

"It's different!" I said loudly. "Trust me!"

But when I sat down in church, I got to thinking. The way Rose put it, our Sundays in the park sounded just as same old, same old as our Sundays in church. So why didn't they *feel* that way?

It's like I said, I thought. *They're different.*

But the more I thought, the more alike both things seemed to be. At the park, we did the same things over because they made us feel close as a family. Wasn't Mass like that, too? Weren't we doing the same things each week so we could get closer to our church family and to God?

At the park we shared a meal together. Even though we ate pretty much the same thing every time, it was special to us. And at church we always shared Holy Communion. That was a meal, too. So what *was* the difference between church and our family outings?

The first Communion kids started filing in. I looked back and found Rose in the line, and my thoughts turned to her super-excited attitude about receiving her first Communion. Suddenly I realized that Rose had answered my question before I even asked it. Holy Communion *was* a meal, but it wasn't an *ordinary* meal. It was the most special meal of all because we were receiving Jesus!

I'd been thinking of church as same old, same old, but that wasn't the problem at all. *I* was the problem—me and my attitude. Which needed a major adjustment!

Rose walked calmly past our pew, but I knew she was bursting with excitement. She wasn't going to be daydreaming—not for one second.

And neither was I. How could I zone out now that it had all started to mean something so real to me, too?

As the Mass began, I said a quick prayer. I promised to try not to take something so important for granted again. It wouldn't be easy to change, but I was determined to face the same old, same old of church with a brand-new, brand-new attitude!

Questions to Think and Talk About

Same Old, Same Old

1. Callie's sister helped her look at things differently. How have other people inspired you to change your attitude about something?

2. Describe an activity you never get tired of even though you do it over and over. Why do you like the activity so much?

3. What memories do you have of your first Communion? What is your attitude toward the Eucharist now?

4. What special times do you share with your family? What special times do you share with your church family?

Nothing
to Learn

I couldn't stand out in the hall forever. Mrs. Stefano would wonder where I was. She might even call my real teacher, Mr. Lewis, and ask about me. Then I'd be in trouble. With a sigh, I trudged into the second-grade classroom.

"Hello," said Mrs. Stefano. "Are you Brett?"

"Yes, ma'am," I muttered, my face burning red. All the little kids were staring!

"We're so glad to have you join us," she said. Then she told me to take the desk by the door, where anybody passing by could see me.

There was a booklet about first Communion on the desk. I opened it and used it to hide my face. I had never been so embarrassed in all my life.

First Communion! At my age! When we lived overseas, my parents wanted to delay my first Communion until we returned to America. That way all our family could attend. I never dreamed it would work out like this: a fourth-grader preparing for first Communion with a bunch of second-graders!

Mrs. Stefano talked about the Last Supper, but I didn't listen. Maybe the second-graders needed to learn that stuff, but I already knew it.

And I didn't need the other kids to read paragraphs aloud. I could have read the whole booklet by myself in less time.

After the section about the Last Supper, there were some easy questions to answer. I dashed them off, and Mrs. Stefano said I could go. "See you next Wednesday!" she called after me.

I sneaked into my classroom through the back door and hurried to my desk. In my rush, I crashed into a table. Everybody stared as I stumbled into my seat.

"Where were you?" whispered my friend Andy.

"Nowhere," I snapped.

"Whatever." He was annoyed, I could tell, but he wouldn't bug me. Andy isn't pushy like that.

Unfortunately, some other kids are. At lunch, several people asked where I went. "None of your business," I replied.

The next Wednesday, I slipped out of the room before Mr. Lewis could say anything embarrassing like, "Time to go to second grade, Brett." Mrs. Stefano wasted my time teaching how the Eucharist is really Jesus. Like I didn't know that! After I answered the follow-up questions, I tried to escape quickly.

"Take your booklet home to study," said Mrs. Stefano.

My heart dropped, but I said, "Yes, ma'am."

I slunk into my classroom with the booklet hidden under my arm. Then I dropped it twice while I was trying to stuff it in my desk. When I finally got rid of it, Andy asked, "What was that?"

"What?"

He rolled his eyes. "Never mind."

Which is what I told the people who asked me where I was. I hated being questioned like that!

I asked my parents to get me out of Mrs. Stefano's class, but they just didn't understand.

"Why should you be embarrassed?" asked Mom. "You're not really in second grade."

"And you're learning something important," said Dad.

"Explain that to your friends," said Mom. "They'll understand."

Yeah, right! I thought.

I even tried answering all the questions in my booklet so Mrs. Stefano could see I had nothing to learn about Communion. But when I showed her the booklet, she said, "That's great, Brett. But these questions are just part of our preparations. You still need to be here next Wednesday."

So I was stuck with all these easy lessons I didn't need. My parents had been talking about my first Communion for years, okay? Mrs. Stefano didn't have to tell me it was a special occasion and the beginning of a deeper relationship with God and all that.

When we started practicing in the church, I had to walk through school in a line of second-graders. I hunched over so I would blend in, just in case any of my classmates came along. Since I couldn't see well that way, I kept bumping into the little kids in front of me and tripping over stuff. I felt so stupid!

Mrs. Stefano made us practice filing into the church over and over. I hated the idea of towering over everyone else like a giraffe, so I tried to be inconspicuous in church, too. But with my head down, I kept walking past my pew. Which meant we had to keep practicing!

Two days before the big event, a terrible storm damaged the church's roof and flooded part of our school. Instead of canceling everything (I was so wishing he would!) Father Denny arranged to hold the first Communion Mass in the gym down the street.

I couldn't believe I went through all that grief just to start my new relationship with God in a gym. Gee, how special.

My entire family came to see my first Communion. Before the sacrament, we all met up in the run-down gym. I was embarrassed that everything looked so awful, but nobody said anything. They were too busy hugging me to death, I guess.

I got a big shock when Andy appeared at my elbow and said hi. "Wh-what are you doing here?" I asked.

"It's my cousin's first Communion," he said. "What about you?"

He'd know the truth soon anyway so I mumbled, "Mine, too."

"That's great, Brett!"

"Really?"

"Sure!" he said. "Communion helps you get closer to God. You'll see! Oops! Dad's waving at me. Talk to you later."

For a minute, I just stood there, thinking. All around me I saw joyful faces. You'd never know our church and school were a mess. And nobody cared that we were in some dingy old gym—not even my relatives, who had waited so long for this day. Everybody acted as if nothing could spoil this special event.

At that moment, I felt ashamed of myself. I'd been so wrapped up in unimportant things that I lost track of what really mattered. Andy was right: this was a special day. And the beginning of a new phase in my relationship with God. Which was really amazing! (Mrs. Stefano tried to teach me that, but I wasn't willing to learn, was I?) I should have been treasuring this time, not worrying about stuff like how easy the reading material was or what my classmates thought.

Father announced that all the first communicants should meet in the lobby, so I went to take my place in line. *I'm sorry about my bad attitude, Lord,* I prayed as I waited for things to start. *But I've learned better now.*

When I marched in with the second-graders, my heart was open and my head was high.

I didn't mess up even once. I guess that's because I could really see where I was going!

Questions to Think and Talk About

Nothing to Learn

1. Brett thought he already knew everything about the Eucharist, but studying our faith is a lifelong process. What have you learned about your faith recently?

2. How do you think Brett's classmates would have reacted if they found out where he was going? How could he have handled their reactions?

3. Tell about a time you were embarrassed. How do you feel about the incident now?

4. Why is it important to study and prepare for receiving the sacraments?

Seriously?

Don't get me wrong. I think my friend Z is hilarious. He's been cracking me up ever since he walked into kindergarten wearing a fake moustache. But some things in life aren't a joke. Like Confirmation.

Which anybody could tell from our very first meeting about the sacrament. All the kids in my grade attended along with their parents. This was one meeting nobody wanted to miss!

Z and his mom sat down next to me and my parents, and I said, "Hey, Z."

"Hey, Meinrad." Z had recently decided my name was boring, and he kept trying to get me to change it.

"Call me Bob," I told him for the hundredth time.

Father Franco got up and gave a talk about the importance of Confirmation. Then our religion teacher, Mrs. Rush, spoke about what we'd be learning in our classes. After that, the principal discussed the requirements for being confirmed. Confirmation was obviously a big deal!

But I looked over and saw that Z was doing his famous bored-to-death act. That's where he yawns and yawns then suddenly slumps in his seat with his tongue hanging out. I normally find it funny, but this time I was annoyed. And so was his mother.

"Straighten up, Zebediah!" she hissed.

He sat up and folded his arms, looking mad. It bugs him to be called by his own un-boring name.

When the meeting was over, Z's mom turned to my parents. "My sister's kids weren't confirmed until they were fifteen. Maybe it's better to wait until they're older." She glared at Z. "And ready to take it seriously."

Z looked embarrassed. "I was just joking."

"I bet Z is ready to show the proper attitude," said my dad.

"I am!" said Z.

But Z's mom looked pretty doubtful as they left. Which was how I felt, too.

"I don't think Z's ready for Confirmation," I told my parents after we got into the car.

"Well, he has lots of time to study and prepare," said Mom.

"And really think things through," said Dad.

It was like they'd never even met Z. Sure, he could get serious for a while—like during Mass—but we were talking some serious seriousness here. Preparing for Confirmation took months and months. I just didn't think Z could handle it.

Soon he started proving me right. In our first class about Confirmation, Mrs. Rush explained that our parents chose Christianity for us at

Baptism. "But at your Confirmation, you make a personal commitment to your faith," she said. "You decide . . . not your parents."

"Seriously?" said Z. "But I have trouble deciding what socks to wear."

Everyone laughed, but Mrs. Rush said, "That's why we spend a long time preparing for this sacrament. We want to be sure you're ready."

"Thanks!" said Z, pretending to be sincere.

"You're welcome," said Mrs. Rush as if she really meant it.

Out in the hall afterward, I told Z, "You don't fool me, you know."

He put on a puzzled face and said, "Okay."

One afternoon a few days later, I went to Z's house to see if he wanted to go to the park. When I walked into his room, he had our religion book open on his desk, and he was acting like he was studying the chapter Mrs. Rush had assigned for homework.

"Oh, hey, Ferdinand," he said, acting surprised.

"Like you didn't see me coming," I said. "And call me Bob. Want to shoot some hoops?"

"Okay," he said, bookmarking the page as if he would be studying more later.

Mrs. Rush talked a lot at our next class, but I didn't pay attention until she asked Z to name the effects of Confirmation. To my amazement, he took a deep breath, then quickly answered, "Strengthens relationship with God unites us to Christ increases gifts of Holy Spirit makes us adult members of Church gives us strength to—" he gasped then added, "proclaim the faith!"

The other kids all laughed, but I didn't think he was funny. I mean . . . memorizing important stuff like that just so you can clown around in class? That is so lame.

"Good!" said Mrs. Rush. Then she looked at me. "Bob, can you name the gifts of the Holy Spirit?"

I hadn't even looked at our assignment! "I . . . um . . . didn't study . . . enough."

"Maybe this is a good time for me to remind everyone that you're making an important decision about your faith," said Mrs. Rush. "So you need to take your studies seriously."

I felt embarrassed—and kind of mad, too. Why should I get in trouble when Z was the one with the sorry attitude?

Mrs. Rush talked about our service requirements next. "Helping others is an important part of really living your faith," she said. "That's why you're required to do twenty-five hours of service before your Confirmation."

"Is that all?" asked Z, like a smart aleck.

Mrs. Rush answered him seriously. "Yes, but you can always do more on your own."

We talked about a number of possible service projects. Mrs. Rush said we could do any of those activities and then passed out a form for keeping track of our service hours.

"I can call the nursing home and arrange for some of you to visit on Saturday," she said. "Who would like to go?"

Z waved his hand in the air. "I'll do it!" He looked at me and added, "And so will Franklin, right?"

"It's Bob," I said. "And, okay, I'll go."

"Great!" said Z. "This will be fun!"

He was so enthusiastic, I knew he had to be kidding around. I thought a bit and realized he was probably just looking for a new audience who didn't know all his routines. He didn't care about service—he was just taking his act on the road!

After class, I said, "Can't you ever be serious about anything?"

He gave me a very serious look then said in a very serious voice, "What do you mean, Cornelius?"

"Call me Bob," I said through gritted teeth. "And you're not funny." Then I walked off.

After that, I didn't give the nursing home another thought until Friday night. My cousin Joe called to see if I could go fishing the next morning. That's when I remembered the service project. But I had a lot of time to get in my service hours, and I really didn't want to watch Z goofing around at the nursing home anyway, so I told Joe I could go.

When Z and I met up outside church after the Saturday evening Mass, he said, "I was cracking people up all over that nursing home! You should have been there, Ichabod. First, I did that thing where I—"

"You know, Z," I interrupted, "the service projects aren't about you."

He frowned. "What are you talking about?"

"They're serious!" I cried. "But you don't know what that means, do you? Every moment is just another chance for you to horse around. You can't even take Confirmation seriously." And because I was sick of his name game, I added, "Zebediah!"

His eyes blazed. "You think *I'm* not taking Confirmation seriously? What about you?"

"I'm serious!" I cried.

He snorted. "Right. You don't pay attention in class. You don't study. And where were you this morning?"

I didn't want to answer that so I said nothing.

"Look," he said. "I fool around a lot, but I know when something is important, too. And confirming my faith . . . that means a lot."

Then he went and stood by his mom, who was talking to my parents.

I had never seen Z look so dead serious. I didn't know he had it in him. I had just assumed he was joking about all the Confirmation stuff, but looking back I realized I must have taken everything the wrong way. I didn't even give Z a chance.

And who was I to criticize him anyway? I talked a good game, but when it came right down to it, how serious had *I* been acting? Confirmation's about promising to live the faith, but I couldn't even commit to getting ready for the sacrament. Z was so right about me!

Which is what I told him once I got him to move away from our parents. I took a deep breath and, before I could chicken out, I quickly said, "You were right I was wrong I shouldn't have said that stuff I'm sorry!"

Z laughed and said, "It's okay," then he added, "Robert."

"Call me . . . " I smiled as I realized what he'd just said. "Close enough!"

Since then I've changed how I'm dealing with Confirmation. I'm trying to be just as serious as Z. (Okay, there's something I never thought I'd ever say.) I really do care about my faith, and now I'm working hard to get ready to receive the sacrament.

I've changed my attitude toward Z, too. Oh, he still makes me laugh, but now I know there's more to him than I thought. Seriously!

Questions to Think and Talk About

Seriously?

1. What would people be surprised to learn about you? Why don't they know about it already?

2. Bob couldn't name the gifts of the Holy Spirit. Can you?

3. Tell about a time you misunderstood someone's actions. What caused the misunderstanding, and how did you come to realize the truth?

4. Why should we have a serious attitude about the sacraments?

Broken

Hey, I'm no angel. I've done things that I shouldn't have. But this time was different. This time I did something really terrible.

It started when I joined the after-school swimming program downtown. There were kids there from all over—including Adam Weber, the most popular guy at my school.

"Hey, Dave," he said when he saw me.

"Hey," I said back. And . . . well . . . that was it.

But the next day Adam came up to me at school and said, "What a workout, huh?"

"Yeah. Really," I replied.

"Later," he said, walking on.

"Whoa," said my best friend, Brody. "Since when do you know Adam Weber?"

"We've known him since second grade," I pointed out.

"Yeah, but not to talk to."

"Well, we're both in swimming now," I told him.

"Gee, Dave, I guess I'm lucky you're even speaking to a nobody like me," teased Brody.

I laughed. "I like to keep in touch with the *little* people, you know."

Brody's the shortest guy in our grade, but he laughed, too. When you've been best friends for years, you can joke around like that. I always thought nothing could break up our friendship.

But things began to change. Adam and I got to know each other better, and we started talking more at school. Usually Brody just stood there, ping-ponging his head between us. Which was fine. But then he had to go and open his mouth!

Like one time Adam and I were talking about building upper body strength for swimming, and I said, "We should do push-ups."

And Adam said, "Right, and—"

"Weights are good, too," interrupted Brody. Then he flexed his skinny arms like a body builder and went, "NYAARRRR!"

Luckily, the bell rang before he could embarrass me anymore. Well . . . for the moment.

Another time, Brody came up to Adam and me and yelled, "Hey, dudes! What's happening?" Then he grinned at us and bobbed his head up and down.

Adam rolled his eyes and told me, "I'll talk to you later." And walked off!

How could I ever get a real friendship going with Adam as long as Brody hung around acting like a dweeb? Every morning before school I prayed, *Please, Lord, make Brody cool. Or absent*. And every day, he showed up and embarrassed me again!

"That Brady kid is annoying," Adam told me at swimming one day.

I couldn't really disagree with that, so I just said, "His name is Brody."

One time I told Brody to meet me at the library but left him waiting, just so I could talk to Adam without him wrecking things. Then I lied and said I had forgotten about our plan. I felt bad about that, so on Saturday, when my family went to Reconciliation, I confessed the lie. Then I promised myself—and God—that I wouldn't lie to my friend anymore.

But being honest with Brody didn't help the situation. Like one time when Adam had just walked off, I told Brody, "Two's company, three's a crowd. Know what I mean?"

Brody got serious. "Yeah, but let's not say anything, okay, Dave? I don't want to hurt Adam's feelings."

My problem got even worse when the grading period ended. On our new schedules, Adam had the same lunchtime as Brody and me. The first day of the change, Adam and I were talking before school and he said, "So . . . see you at lunch?"

"Sure." I acted casual, but inside I was thinking, *Yes! I'm finally going to be part of the popular group!*

If I could keep Brody from ruining things! I managed to escape him at lunchtime and get into the cafeteria line behind Adam and his friends. Hopefully, we'd be seated before Brody caught up. I was planning to make sure there were no empty chairs anywhere near me.

Later I'd have to have a talk with Brody about getting lost when Adam was around. But for now, I just needed to make it through today's lunch.

But I didn't. Brody appeared at my elbow and shouted, "I found you guys!"

"Give me a break," muttered Adam. Then he frowned at *me*! Like maybe he was thinking I wasn't worth the trouble of having Brody hanging around.

I had to act quickly. "No cuts," I said, hoping Brody would move on. But he just laughed and tried to push in front of me. I could see there was only one way to get rid of him. "Sheesh, Brody," I said, "do you have to be such a leech? Get a clue, why don't you?"

The smile dropped off his face, and he slowly walked to the end of the line.

Adam snorted. "I think he finally got the message."

"Yeah," I said. "And it's about time."

I thought it would be so cool to eat lunch with the popular kids, but I couldn't enjoy the moment at all—thanks to Brody! It made me mad that he was so dense. I mean . . . he practically forced me to hurt his feelings.

Of course I felt sorry for him, even though the whole thing was his own fault. But I figured he'd get over it. After all, we'd been friends forever. A little thing like this wasn't going to break us apart.

But for three days, Brody wouldn't even look at me. He ignored anything I said, and he walked right past me in the halls. He wouldn't even come to the phone when I called.

I told myself I didn't care, since I had plenty of new friends with Adam and his group. But it bugged me that Brody was making something out of nothing. By Saturday I was sick of the situation, and I went over to his house to have it out. I found him outside, shooting hoops.

He tucked the basketball under his arm and said, "What do you want?"

"I get it that you're mad about what happened at lunch the other day. But it really wasn't a big deal."

"Not a big deal?" he shouted. "You stabbed me in the back—in front of everybody!"

I had never seen Brody so angry. And the look in his eyes . . . he was hurting. Because of me! I tried to work myself up and get mad at him again, but all the excuses I'd been making for myself seemed pretty lame now. Finally, I mumbled, "Well, you just wouldn't take a hint."

"Here's a hint for *you*," he said. "Go away!"

"I'm sorry, okay?" I yelled.

"So? That doesn't make everything right." He turned back to the basketball hoop.

I couldn't argue with that, so I went home. I didn't blame Brody for not forgiving me—I had broken up our friendship over nothing, really. Like being in the popular group was worth hurting somebody on purpose. Hey, *I* wouldn't forgive me either.

For the next week, I hung out with Adam and his friends, but I didn't talk much. One time Brody passed our table when there was an empty seat right next to me. I almost told him he could sit there, but then I chickened out and let him walk by.

My heart felt like a boulder, and I got so tired of hauling it around. But what could I do? I didn't see any point in even trying to fix things. Obviously our friendship was broken for good!

That Saturday, I asked my mom to take me to Reconciliation again. Betraying my friend was the worst thing I'd ever done, and the idea of confessing it just made my heart feel heavier. But I knew I had to do it. Once I told Father Chang what I'd done, I felt a little better. I said my Act of Contrition and really meant it. Then Father encouraged me to make up with Brody, gave me some prayers for penance, and said the words of absolution.

That's when the weight lifted off my heart, and I felt a *lot* better. To know I had God's forgiveness, even if I didn't have Brody's, was such a relief.

Of course, I still wanted to be friends with Brody again. After I said my penance, I asked God to help me figure out what to do. The thought came to me that I had only apologized to Brody one time—and not very well. He deserved more than that! I decided I would give him a real apology. It might not work, but I had to at least *try* to repair our friendship.

And now I felt I had the power to handle the job. That came from God, I knew. It was like things got broken between us, too, when I treated my friend like that. And I was pretty shaky without God! Then the sacrament brought me back to him, and that made me stronger—strong enough to do the right thing.

I was pretty hopeful that Brody would forgive me some day. And if he did, I was determined that nothing would ever break us apart again. That went for God and me, too!

Questions to Think and Talk About

Broken

1. How can you tell Dave was truly sorry for hurting Brody?

2. Forgiveness is one of God's greatest gifts—and it's something we can share with others. When have you shown forgiveness? How could you be more forgiving?

3. Receiving the sacrament of Reconciliation gave Dave the strength to do the right thing. What other benefits do we get from the sacrament?

4. Do you think Dave should stay friends with Adam? Why or why not?

Out of the
Maze

"They're beautiful," said Mom, "but way too expensive."

"All the girls at my new school wear earrings like this!" I cried.

"I'm sorry, Avril," said Mom, returning the earrings to the rack. "We can't afford them." Then she walked away to look at a display of socks.

At that moment, I hated being the new girl. I didn't have any friends yet—and I figured I never would until I fit in with the styles. If I just had those earrings . . .

My hand shot out, plucked the earrings off the rack, and slipped them into my pocket!

Why did I do that? I asked myself as Mom led the way out of the store. The latest jewelry couldn't fix my social life—I had to make friends for myself. And stealing was wrong!

When we got home, I hid the earrings in my dresser and tried to forget about them. But I couldn't do it. They were on my mind all night long—and for days after that. Every time I saw other girls in my class wearing earrings, I was reminded of what I'd done. And I couldn't stop thinking about how disappointed Mom would be if she knew I'd taken them.

It really bothered me to have committed such a serious sin. Back in our old town, I would have gone to confession, which always made me feel better. The first time I received the sacrament of Reconciliation was from Father Stephen, our pastor there—and all the times after that, too. He'd known me since I was a little kid, and I was really comfortable with him.

But I hardly knew the priest at our new church. Mom and I met Father Brandt when we registered in the church office, and he seemed very nice. But I was a total stranger to him. If the first confession he heard from me was about stealing, he'd think I was an awful person!

I worried and worried about the situation. It was like being lost in a carnival maze . . . you know . . . the ones made of glass and mirrors? No matter which way I turned my thoughts, I couldn't figure a way out. I wanted to confess and receive God's forgiveness. But to do that, I had to show Father Brandt my bad side. So maybe I shouldn't go to Reconciliation. But I wouldn't feel right until I did! So I *had* to confess my sin. But if I did that . . . AAARGH!

One night I was lying in bed, wandering around the maze in my mind, when I finally realized what I needed to do. I had to stay away from Reconciliation until Father Brandt formed a really good impression of me. Then when I made my confession, the whole stealing thing would just seem like a little slip-up—and I wouldn't look so bad!

I put my plan into action at Mass on Sunday. I asked Mom if we could sit right up front in church. Then I made sure to sing loudly, join in all the responses, and look as holy as possible. I couldn't tell if Father Brandt noticed me or not. He did smile as we shook hands after the service, but he smiled at everyone, so that didn't mean anything.

A few days later, Father Brandt dropped by our classroom, and I got another chance to impress him. I sat up straight. I raised my hand for every question. And when we started our assignment, I wrote extra neatly in case he walked by. But when I looked up, Father had already slipped out of the room. Who knew if he even saw me?

"You have really nice handwriting," said Naomi, the girl who sits next to me.

"Thanks," I said with a sigh.

At lunch, Naomi and some of the other girls were talking about youth group, which was meeting that night. I just sat there, eating my lunch and not talking, as usual. Then Naomi turned to me and said, "You should come to the meeting, Avril."

"Yeah!" said the others.

"Okay," I said. "I will!" It was the second time people had acted friendly to me in one day. That made me feel hopeful about things working out at school, but I was still worried about my other problem. How long was it going to take for Father Brandt to get to know my good side?

Luckily, he came to youth group that night. I acted especially reverent when he led us in the opening prayer. Then, during the business part of the meeting, I volunteered to visit the nursing home, sell cookies after Mass, bring in canned goods, make get-well cards for sick parishioners, and pray every day for world peace. How could Father not be impressed with me?

During refreshment time, he came up and asked me, "How are things going for you, Avril?"

"Fine!" I peeped.

"Good," he said. "We're so glad to have you and your mother join our community." Then he moved on without saying one word about all the good stuff I just did!

The rest of the evening should have been fun, since we were playing games, but my heart just wasn't in it. I couldn't wait forever to be free of my sin, but now I realized my stupid plan was going to take at least that long to work!

That night I lay awake a long time, feeling hopelessly lost. How was I ever going to get out of the mess I was in? Finally, I had to admit the truth. It was time to get some guts and go to confession. Until I did that, I'd never escape the maze my life had become.

So on Friday afternoon I went to the church for Reconciliation. As I waited my turn, I kept telling myself that everything would be okay— and I actually started to believe that!

Until a new thought suddenly appeared out of nowhere like one of those tricky glass walls in a maze. What if Father Brandt did things differently from Father Stephen? Father Stephen always gave a penance, of course, but maybe Father Brandt wouldn't think that was enough—especially for something serious like stealing. He might make me tell the store manager that I'd stolen the earrings! Or maybe I would have to confess to Mom, too!

I tried to remember what I learned about Reconciliation when I first received the sacrament. There was something about the seal of confession, but didn't that just mean the priest couldn't tell anybody what I said? It didn't have anything to do with telling on myself, did it? And maybe I *should* tell other people. But if I did . . . AAARGH!

I was all confused again! And scared, too. I wanted to walk out and forget the whole thing, but I took a breath and prayed a while instead. I asked God to help me, and, when my turn came, I was able to stand up and go to the Reconciliation room.

Reconciliation went pretty much the same as it had at my old church. After I confessed my sins and said my Act of Contrition, Father gave me some prayers for penance and explained that I also needed to return what I had stolen. Then he said the words of absolution. Usually

I feel really relieved at that point, but I couldn't relax just yet.

"Father?" I swallowed hard. "Am I supposed to tell other people that I stole something?"

"No, Avril," he said kindly. "Confessions are sealed. That means I will never speak of what you've told me, and you don't need to say anything either. Unless you *want* to talk about it."

It felt so good to hear that!

"It's important to make up for your sin by returning what you stole," he added. "But telling anyone else is entirely up to you."

"I'll return them right away," I promised. Mom and I were going back to the mall this weekend. When no one was looking, I could leave the earrings on the counter. And I'd think about whether I might want to talk to Mom about it, too.

Father smiled. "I don't know you very well, Avril, but I can tell you love God and want to do the right thing. That's wonderful."

When he said that, I realized something. I had worried so much about making a bad impression on Father Brandt, but receiving the sacrament actually showed him my good side. He didn't think I was a terrible person at all!

I thanked Father then went back into the church and said my penance. After that, I sat and thought a bit. Staying away from Reconciliation had been a big mistake—I could see that now. In a way, it was like staying away from God. No wonder I got so mixed up.

But after receiving Reconciliation, things seemed much clearer—like I was on the right track again. For the moment! I'll mess up again sometime, of course, but at least now I know what to do about it. The next time I lose my way, I'm using the sacraments to get back to God!

Questions to Think and Talk About

Out of the Maze

1. Has anyone ever gotten the wrong impression of you? What did you do about it?

2. Receiving the sacraments brings us closer to God. What are some other things we can do to grow closer with God?

3. Should Avril tell her mother about stealing the earrings? Why or why not?

4. Sometimes people feel nervous about receiving Reconciliation. What concerns do you have about the sacrament?

Full of Life

"Hmphf."

Doctor Robertson made that noise several times during my physical, but I didn't think anything of it. He was a new doctor, and, for all I knew, he did that all the time.

But I got worried when he said, "Would you go to the waiting room, Sophie? I'd like to speak to your mother."

I plopped onto a sofa and prayed there wasn't a problem. For the first time, I was trying out for a sport, and I needed Doctor Robertson's permission.

When Mom finally came out, I jumped up. "Well? Do I get to run track?"

"We don't know yet," she said. "The doctor wants to do some tests to be sure you can handle it."

Sometimes when I ran, I got breathless and my legs hurt. That was why I wanted to join track—to get into shape. "Practice starts soon," I complained. "I hope this doesn't take long."

But I missed the first few weeks of track because I had to go to special doctors and give samples of blood and have images taken of my heart and a million other things. Finally, my parents went to see Doctor Robertson about my results.

When they walked into the house afterward, I could tell they had bad news. "Let's sit down," said Dad, looking serious.

They started talking, but at first I didn't get what they were saying. Then it hit me. "Are you telling me there's something wrong with my heart?" I cried.

"Not your heart," said Mom. "It's the big blood vessel that comes from your heart—the aorta." She explained my aorta had a narrow part that wouldn't let blood go through properly.

"Some people are just born that way," said Dad.

"The good news is the doctors can do something about it," said Mom.

"Like what?" I asked.

When they told me I would need surgery, my heart started pounding. "You mean . . . they'll cut into me?"

Mom hugged me from one side as Dad hugged me from the other.

"I know you have a lot of concerns. And questions," said Dad. "So do we."

"We made an appointment with Doctor Chan, the specialist who'll do the surgery. We'll all go and ask her about everything," said Mom. "In the meantime, try not to worry, okay?"

Then Dad led us in prayer, asking God to help us deal with the situation. I'd like to say that calmed me down, but I was too upset to feel better.

The meeting with Doctor Chan didn't help either. She said she'd keep my incision as small as possible, but a cut is a cut, okay? Then she explained, "I'll take out the narrow part of the artery and sew the good parts together. You'll be sedated, so you won't feel anything."

"But what about after I wake up?" I asked.

"I have to be honest," she said. "You'll have some discomfort. But we can give you pain medication to help with that. You'll feel better in a week or two, but it will be a while before you can resume normal activities."

She went on to talk about how I would be able to exercise later, but I was too worried about the pain to care. How bad would I be hurting? And what if I couldn't handle it? I was really nervous, but I tried to act cool about everything.

But when my parents and I got into our car afterward, I burst into tears. Dad hopped into the back seat to hug me, and Mom kept handing me tissues until I finally got hold of myself. Then I hiccupped out, "It's . . . going . . . to . . . hurt!"

"Yes, it will hurt some," said Mom. "But Doctor Chan is an excellent surgeon, and she's done a lot of these procedures. She'll be sure that it hurts as little as possible."

"And the nurses will give you medication to help with the pain," said Dad. "Okay?"

I nodded, but I didn't actually feel any better. All my parents were saying was that my surgery would not be pain-free!

Mom and Dad let me stay home from school the next few days. I was really glad because I felt like I'd cry if I had to talk to my friends about the surgery. But one night Mom answered the phone, then held it out and said, "It's Kat."

I didn't want to talk to anybody—even my best friend—but I couldn't say that with the phone two inches from my face! So I took it and said, "Hi, Kat."

"How are you?" she asked. "Are you nervous about your surgery?"

"How . . . how did you know about that?"

"I talked to your dad on the phone yesterday," she said. "Listen . . . I want you to know everybody is praying for you."

Tears came to my eyes. "Thanks," I whispered. Then I had to hang up.

It was nice of my friends to pray for me, and that made me feel better for a while. But when I was lying in bed that night, I got all scared again—so scared that I couldn't pray myself. I hated to be such a chicken, but I didn't want to suffer!

My parents kept trying to reassure me. They showed me information on the Internet—as if knowing more would make the surgery hurt less. They talked about what a miracle it was that my problem could be corrected—unlike in the olden days. But when I thought about being in pain, I couldn't make myself care about those poor pioneer kids. My parents even invited my grandparents over for supper two nights before my surgery so they could talk about all the operations they'd ever had.

"Didn't hurt at all!" said Grandpa.

"Well, not much," said Grandma.

"Not that much," said Grandpa.

"Not as much as you might think," said Grandma.

"Mother, Father . . . how about some more mashed potatoes?" said Mom.

After my grandparents left, Dad said, "You're still worried, aren't you?"

I nodded. "I'm sorry."

"You don't need to apologize," said Mom. "What you're feeling is completely natural."

"I just wish there was a way for you to feel better," said Dad.

"Hmphf," said Mom, sounding like Doctor Robertson. "Maybe there is." But she didn't say anything else.

The next afternoon—which was the day before my surgery—Father Mike dropped by for a visit. We all chatted a bit in the living room, then he turned to me and said, "I understand you're worried about your surgery."

I nodded. "I don't want to be afraid, but . . . well . . . I am."

"I understand," he said. "God can help you through this hard time, Sophie. You know about Anointing of the Sick, don't you?"

"Yes, it's one of the seven sacraments, the ones Jesus gave us." Suddenly I felt scared. Was I in worse shape than I thought? "Isn't it for people who are extremely ill?"

"Sometimes it's given to people in danger of dying, but Anointing of the Sick is a sacrament full of life," said Father. "It brings grace to any seriously ill person. The Holy Spirit blesses the sick person in body and soul and gives them strength and courage to deal with all the difficulties of illness."

"Wow," I said. "I could use that kind of help."

"I'm prepared to give you the sacrament right now if you want it," said Father.

So this was Mom's big idea! I looked at her and smiled. Then I turned back to Father Mike and said, "Yes. I'd like to receive the sacrament."

Father opened a small box he had brought with him, took out a stole, and placed it around his neck. Then he sprinkled around some holy water with a little metal sprinkler from the box. After that, he led us in prayer and read from the Bible. Then we were all silent for a while.

I really felt God's love in that quiet moment—and through the rest of the sacrament, too. I felt it when Father anointed my forehead and hands with sacred oil. I felt it when he asked God to bless me and give me strength. I felt it when we all said the Lord's Prayer and received Holy Communion.

The whole thing didn't last long, but it made a huge difference! I knew I could face my surgery because God had made me strong enough to deal with the pain—and whatever else might happen. I had courage from the Holy Spirit—and peacefulness inside. Maybe my body needed some work, but I felt really good in my soul.

That feeling lasted all the way up to my surgery, and afterward, too. There was pain, and . . . well . . . it hurt! But it wasn't as bad as I was afraid it would be, and I handled it, with God's help.

Now I'm at home, and I still feel strong inside even though my body needs some more recovery time. Father Mike was right when he called the anointing a sacrament full of life. Soon I'll be ready to do a lot of living!

Questions to Think and Talk About

Full of Life

1. God is always with us, but sometimes we sense his presence more strongly. Tell about a time you felt close to God.

2. How have your parents or other family members supported you through your problems?

3. It can be hard to pray when we're feeling troubled, but that's the time we need God the most! What should a person do if prayer is difficult?

4. Anointing of the Sick reminds us that Jesus healed many people, both physically and spiritually. How was Sophie healed by the sacrament?

The Worst Wedding Ever!

"What about pink?" I asked.

Mom frowned. "Oh, Amber. You know your sister doesn't like pink."

Jenna, the big sister who wasn't getting married, said, "Besides, it's a fall wedding. Pink isn't a fall color."

Tori, the sister who *was* getting married, said, "I'm using these colors for my wedding." She laid three fabric squares on the kitchen table.

I couldn't believe what I was seeing. "Your colors are brown, purple, and orange?"

"That's chocolate, eggplant, and peach," said Mom.

"But those are foods," I said. "Not colors for a wedding. A lot of people won't like them." *Including me!* I thought.

"That's okay. I love them," said Tori. "And so does Jake." Jake was Tori's fiancé. For a long time we wondered if they were ever going to get engaged.

Mom and Jenna liked the colors, too, so I didn't say anything more. If Tori wanted disgusting colors for her wedding, that was her decision.

She got to decide about the bridesmaids' dresses, too, of course. I was a junior brides- maid. Which sounded cool, until I tried on my dress at the bridal shop.

"That peach color is beautiful!" cried Mom as I came out of the dressing room.

"It's orange," I said. "And what's with all the ruffles? You know, the bride magazine said ruffles are out."

"I don't care, because you look fantastic!" said Tori. "That color will really complement Ronnie's brown tux."

My cousin Ronnie was the junior usher. We would walk down the aisle together. Which was a big mistake, I thought. "Can't I walk in with somebody else? Ronnie's a foot shorter than me! We'll look funny."

"Everybody's paired up," said Mom.

"And Ronnie's with you," said Jenna.

"Don't worry," said Tori. "You'll be cute together."

Mom and Jenna agreed! Was I the only person who realized Tori was messing up her wedding? Okay, *her* off-white gown (which was "cream" according to Mom) looked gorgeous, but everything else was a disaster so far.

And the more Tori planned, the worse things got. Like, she chose carrot cake for her reception.

"Aren't you supposed to have white cakes at weddings?" I asked.

"It's a fall wedding," said Jenna.

"And carrot cake is our favorite," said Tori.

But I just knew everybody would be disappointed to have such an ordinary dessert.

The daisy bouquets were another problem. What's special about flowers I can pick in my own yard?

"Gee," I told Tori, "maybe you should have dandelions, too."

She didn't get my sarcasm. "We can't do that, but we could add some dried yarrow."

I was stunned to find out that yarrow was a yellow flower that looked like a weed!

The centerpieces for the reception were a shock, too. They would be made of leaves and teensy pumpkins!

"Pumpkins!" I cried. "At a wedding reception?"

"It's fall," said Jenna.

Mom said, "And pumpkins are a fall thing." Then she added, "And they cost a lot less than flowers."

"They'll look pretty, Amber," said Tori. "You'll see."

Right, I thought. *There's nothing as beautiful as a pumpkin!*

I tried to get Mom to take some action. "Tori is ruining her wedding," I told her in private.

"What do you mean?" she asked.

I started counting on my fingers. "Number one, her colors are putrid. Number two, the bridesmaids' dresses are ugly. Number Three, carrot cake! Number—"

Mom interrupted before I got to the pumpkins. "This is Tori's wedding—not yours."

"I know," I said, "but don't you think we should tell her the truth?"

Mom frowned. "The truth is that Tori's wedding will be beautiful. And don't you tell her it won't!"

Obviously Mom wouldn't be any help.

Talking to Jenna didn't do any good either. Whenever I complained about something—the colors, the bouquets, the cake, *whatever*—she just said, "It's a fall wedding." Like that made everything okay.

"So maybe we should have jack-o'-lanterns," I told her. "They're a fall thing!"

She looked at me and went, "Hmmmm . . ."

"Just joking!" I cried.

"Me, too," she said with a grin.

Finally I thought of somebody who might be able to straighten Tori out. "So," I asked her one day, "when you and Jake have those meetings with Father Donald, do you discuss the wedding?"

"Sometimes," she said.

"Did you tell him about your cake? And the pumpkins?"

"We're there to talk about our *marriage*," said Tori. "You know . . . to prepare for our life together, for raising our children in the faith, things like that. Father's not concerned about every little detail of our wedding."

Neither are you, I thought. It looked like I was the only person who *did* care!

When Tori told me she was planning to ask Aunt Nadine to sing at the ceremony, I tried one more time to save her wedding. "Aunt Nadine isn't professional," I pointed out. "Sometimes she has trouble with the high notes. A lot of trouble. Like she doesn't even get close."

Tori just laughed. "Oh, Amber! I love Aunt Nadine and I want her to be involved in my wedding. Don't worry. Everything will be fine."

"No, it won't! You're messing . . . um . . ." I took a breath as I remembered Mom's warning. "I mean . . . it's your big day. Aren't you worried about things being perfect?"

"Not really," said Tori.

After that, I just gave up. I felt bad that my sister's wedding was going to be a catastrophe, but what more could I do?

When the actual day finally came, things started going wrong right away. Relatives who visited the bride's waiting room called the bridesmaids' dresses "unusual" and the colors "unique." They never said they liked them! Jake's grandmother had to leave the room because she was allergic to our weedy bouquets. Then we heard Aunt Nadine begin to sing in the church, and it only took five seconds for her to miss a high note. We hadn't even started, and it was already the worst wedding ever!

It didn't get any better after that. Everybody grinned when Ronnie and I came down the aisle. I was so embarrassed! The relatives who did the readings messed up, Aunt Nadine had trouble with every song she sang, and Tori and Jake almost couldn't get the unity candle lit. I felt so sorry for Tori that I couldn't pay attention to Father Donald's homily. By the time we got to the vows, I was ready for the whole thing to be over—and I was sure she felt the same way.

But as Tori and Jake came before the altar, she was smiling. She looked at Jake so joyfully as he made his vows to her. And when it was her turn, tears came to her eyes as she said, "I take you, Jacob, to be my husband. I promise to be true to you in good times and in bad, in sickness and in health. I will love you and honor you all the days of my life."

Wow, I thought. *She's talking about forever.* And my eyes filled, too.

I looked down at my orange ruffles and my weedy little bouquet. I still didn't like them, but that didn't seem so important now. After all, Tori and Jake were making a promise before God. I mean . . . this was a sacrament! I had focused so much on all the wedding preparations, I'd forgotten that.

But Tori didn't. Sure, she wanted her wedding to be beautiful, but she knew it wasn't just a pretty show. That's why she hadn't worried about the wedding details as much as I thought she should. She was more concerned about preparing for a lifetime commitment. All the counseling with Father Donald was about getting ready for that. And, now that I thought about it, maybe waiting to get engaged was, too.

The rest of the wedding went quickly, and soon we were all marching down the aisle and out to the vestibule. I didn't care anymore if people noticed how I dwarfed Ronnie. I wasn't concerned about my dress, the flowers, the reception, or anything else. I was just happy that God had blessed Tori's wedding—and I knew he would bless her marriage, too.

Tori pulled me to her side as we formed the receiving line. "So what did you think?"

I hugged her and told her the truth. "It was beautiful!" I said.

Questions to Think and Talk About

The Worst Wedding Ever!

1. How do you decide whether or not to point out someone's mistakes?

2. Amber worried a lot about her sister's wedding. What kind of things do you worry about? How often do your worries come true?

3. Sometimes we get so involved in life that we forget about God! Tell about a time this happened to you. What made you aware of God's presence again?

4. What commitments have you made? How does God help you keep them?

Could I Do That?

"I want to be a rock star!" shouted my friend Kyle.

I looked up from my desk. Kyle was flopped on my bed, writing in a notebook and listening to music. I signaled for him to drop his earphones then asked, "Why?"

"Sheesh, Ty!" he said. "You sound like Mrs. Emmett."

"Look—you know she'll expect you to give reasons why you picked that career for your paper," I said. "Don't you want a good grade?"

"Okay, okay," he said. "I want to be a rock star to make the world a better place." I rolled my eyes. "Because the money's good?" I shook my head. "Because I'll get to stay up late?"

"We're writing papers about the careers we want when we're adults," I told him. "You'll be able to set your own bedtime then."

"Oh, yeah. Well how about . . . I mean . . ." He sighed. "You're always trying to help me do better, aren't you?" Before I could answer, he added, "That's really annoying, you know."

I laughed and turned to my own paper, which was still completely blank. I had no idea what I wanted to do with *my* life.

When I was little, I always wanted to be a truck driver—not a good job for somebody who gets carsick like I do! I could use it for my paper anyway, but how lame would that be? Surely I could come up with a career that wasn't nauseating.

Luckily, the paper wasn't due for two weeks, so I worked on other stuff until Kyle had to leave. But at supper that night, I started thinking again about my career.

"What do you think I should be when I grow up?" I asked my family.

"Human," said my big sister, Anna.

"Funny," I said.

Mom frowned. "Let's have a nice dinner, please."

"You're a caring person, Ty," said Dad. "So maybe you should be a doctor."

I do like to help people. Even Kyle had said so. "Yeah, I could do that."

"How about becoming a teacher?" suggested Mom.

"I could do that, too," I said. "I guess I'm just not sure what career is right for me."

"You should talk to Uncle Joseph about it," said Anna.

Like Mrs. Emmett, Uncle Joseph asked lots of questions. He really helped you think things through when you had a problem. So my sister had a good idea there.

I shrugged. "Maybe."

"You'd better wait until *after* his big day," said Mom.

Uncle Joseph was becoming a priest, and we were going to his ordination in a few days. I figured he had important stuff on his mind right now. I mean . . . he had decided what to do with *his* life, and he was making it happen.

"I'll talk to him next week," I said. If I hadn't finished my paper by then.

Over the next couple of days, I thought of some possible careers, but nothing seemed quite right. Finally I got an idea at youth group. Our sponsor was late, so I went ahead and passed out our fundraiser candy and filled out the record sheet with how many boxes everybody took. When Mr. Pulaski got there, he said, "I can always count on you, Ty. Good job!"

Hey, maybe I could become some kind of businessman, I thought. I liked the idea of being dependable with paperwork—and money, too. But what kind of business would I do?

Another idea came to me at baseball practice. Coach White was talking about how much we'd improved as a team, and I realized he had a lot to do with that. He really knew how to get us to work together. Wouldn't it be great to be a leader like the coach?

Yeah, I thought. *I could do that!* But then I remembered Coach White was a volunteer—

and so were a lot of other coaches. Not many people did that as a full-time career, did they?

When the day of Uncle Joseph's ordination came, I still hadn't figured anything out. As I walked into the cathedral, I was seriously reconsidering the truck driver thing—and not just for my assignment. I mean . . . what *was* I going to do with my life?

"Isn't this church cool?" Anna whispered to me.

That's when I actually looked around. The cathedral was huge, and it had big marble columns and lots of colorful stained-glass windows. "Yeah," I whispered back.

Uncle Joseph had told us the sacrament of Holy Orders took place in a Mass, but some things would be different. The procession sure was. It was really long because it included Uncle Joseph and the three other men who were being ordained, plus lots of priests and the bishop.

The Mass went on normally until after the Gospel reading. Then the bishop called Uncle Joseph and the other candidates forward, and a priest from their seminary testified that they were ready to become priests. The bishop announced that they were chosen for the priesthood, and everybody applauded. I felt really happy for Uncle Joseph.

But I got nervous for him after the bishop gave his homily and then started to individually question each candidate. It reminded me of getting quizzed by Mrs. Emmett. But then I realized it wasn't like that at all. The candidates were making promises about what they would do as priests. By the time it was Uncle Joseph's turn, I had heard the bishop's questions three times, and I could really concentrate on what they meant.

First, the bishop asked if Uncle Joseph promised to "discharge without fail the office of priesthood," and he replied, "I do." I realized that meant he was promising that people could count on him. Which made me think of what Mr. Pulaski said about me at youth group.

The bishop also asked Uncle Joseph to promise to "celebrate the mysteries of Christ faithfully and religiously." I figured

that was about saying Mass and celebrating
the sacraments—which had to be the most
important things priests did, right? I mean . . .
it's through the sacraments that priests help
people get close to God. Funny—we were just
talking about helping people the other night at
the supper table.

Uncle Joseph also promised to preach the
Gospel and explain the Catholic faith. Talk
about a big responsibility! He was really going
to have to be a good leader, wasn't he? Just the
other day I'd been thinking I'd like leadership
to be part of my job.

Then the bishop asked Uncle Joseph to
consecrate his life to God and to grow closer to
Christ every day. That meant he was actually
giving himself to God! How amazing was that?

That's when another amazing thought hit me.
The priesthood had a lot of what I was looking
for in a career. But I could never be a priest!

Could I?

I watched the rest of the ordination with that
thought on my mind. When all the candidates
lay on the floor during the Litany of Saints, I

wondered if I could ever offer myself to God like that. As the bishop silently laid hands on my uncle, and then all the other priests there did the same, I tried to picture that happening to me. Dressing in vestments . . . being anointed with oil . . . sharing the sign of peace with the bishop and the other priests. . . . Could *I* receive this sacrament one day?

Could I care and teach and lead and give myself to God and celebrate the sacraments and do all the things a priest did? And the most important thing was—what was *God* calling me to do?

After all the special ordination stuff was over, the Mass went on with the Liturgy of the Eucharist, and all the new priests helped out. I noticed a lot of details that I hadn't really paid attention to at Mass before, like the way they poured some water in the chalice with the wine, and how they held the host up when they were giving out the Eucharist.

After Communion, I talked to God about the thoughts that were boiling over in my head. I realized I wasn't ready to make any big decisions about my career. "What are you calling me to be, Lord?" I prayed. "I need you to help me figure this out."

Obviously, I didn't have to choose my life's work just yet, but I did have to decide something about my paper—soon! At least now I had some ideas about some of the things I wanted my career to include. Maybe, I thought, I'd just write about that. Hopefully, Mrs. Emmett would be understanding, as long as I explained why I couldn't choose a specific job yet. I needed time to think. And to pray about it, too.

After Mass, everybody went to a big room for a celebration that included lots of congratulations and plenty of food. As I came back toward my family with my second plate of snacks, I heard Mom ask Uncle Joseph, "Can Ty talk to you sometime in the next few days?"

"He'd like your help with an assignment," explained Dad.

Uncle Joseph spotted me standing nearby. "Hey, Ty. How about we talk tomorrow after-noon?"

I almost said, "Never mind. I'm okay now." But then I realized there were still a lot of things my uncle and I could talk about. Like how did he know God was calling him to the priesthood? And when would I know what God wanted *me* to do?

So I smiled instead and told him, "Sure, I could do that!"

Questions to Think and Talk About

Could I Do That?

1. Our qualities and the things we are interested in can help us to discover what vocation God is calling us to. What are some of the things you would like to do in your life's work?

2. A priest acts in the person of Christ, living a life of service to God's people. What are some ways that priests help your community?

3. What do you do when you're having trouble making a difficult decision?

4. The people in Ty's life thought of him as caring and helpful. How would your family and friends describe you? How would you like to be described?

Anna Mei, Cartoon Girl

By Carol A. Grund

No matter what her name sounds like, Anna Mei is *not* a cartoon character. But she *is* the new kid at school, and that just wasn't in the plan.

How's she ever going to fit in with the other sixth graders when she has a weird name, an adoptive family she doesn't remotely resemble, and an unknown birth mother somewhere back in China? She figures she'd better get busy transforming herself into someone who's less . . . unusual. After all, a pretend life is better than no life. But just when it looks as though Anna Mei 2.0 has everyone fooled, a school project comes along that makes her think about herself, her friends, her family—and that weird name of hers—in a whole new way.

Paperback
144 pp.
07885
$8.95 U.S.

Saints of Note
The Comic Collection

Written by Diana R. Jenkins
Art by Patricia Storms

Join time-travelers Paul and Cecilia as they journey to the past, meet saints, and become inspired to be better people. Their exciting adventures bring the saints to life and make them meaningful for today.

In addition to the comics, you'll also find detailed biographies, fascinating facts, interesting quotes, and other useful material to teach you even more about the saints. You'll enjoy *Saints of Note*, learn a lot—and get inspired, too!

Paperback
96 pp.
71206
$8.95

Who are the Daughters of St. Paul?

We are Catholic sisters. Our mission is to be like Saint Paul and tell everyone about Jesus! There are so many ways for people to communicate with each other. We want to use all of them so everyone will know how much God loves us. We do this by printing books (you're holding one!), making radio shows, singing, helping people at our bookstores, using the Internet, and in many other ways.

Visit our Web site at www.pauline.org

BOOKS & MEDIA

The Daughters of St. Paul operate book and media centers at the following addresses. Visit, call or write the one nearest you today, or find us on the World Wide Web, www.pauline.org

CALIFORNIA
3908 Sepulveda Blvd, Culver City, CA 90230   310-397-8676
2640 Broadway Street, Redwood City, CA 94063   650-369-4230
5945 Balboa Avenue, San Diego, CA 92111   858-565-9181

FLORIDA
145 S.W. 107th Avenue, Miami, FL 33174   305-559-6715

HAWAII
1143 Bishop Street, Honolulu, HI 96813   808-521-2731
Neighbor Islands call: 866-521-2731

ILLINOIS
172 North Michigan Avenue, Chicago, IL 60601   312-346-4228

LOUISIANA
4403 Veterans Memorial Blvd, Metairie, LA 70006   504-887-7631

MASSACHUSETTS
885 Providence Hwy, Dedham, MA 02026   781-326-5385

MISSOURI
9804 Watson Road, St. Louis, MO 63126   314-965-3512

NEW YORK
64 West 38th Street, New York, NY 10018   212-754-1110

PENNSYLVANIA
Philadelphia—relocating   215-969-5068

SOUTH CAROLINA
243 King Street, Charleston, SC 29401   843-577-0175

VIRGINIA
1025 King Street, Alexandria, VA 22314   703-549-3806

CANADA
3022 Dufferin Street, Toronto, ON M6B 3T5   416-781-9131